THE TUTTLE TWINS
and the
12 RULES
BOOT CAMP

To Jordan Peterson

For teaching clarity of thought
and intentional action.

CONNOR BOYACK

Illustrated by Elijah Stanfield

"You two never cease to amaze me!" Grandma Tuttle gushed, as she dished second helpings of her famous peach pie to the twins.

The Tuttle twins were visiting their grandparents' little pink house. Ethan and Emily had just shared a story about one of their recent learning adventures.

"Maybe my latest project will amaze you, too," their Uncle Ben said, his mouth half full. "I've been researching a big story about government corruption that could really make some waves."

"I'm proud of you, Son," Grandpa Tuttle said. "Tuttles do important things. I'm proud of each of you."

Brock, the twins' youngest uncle, suddenly spoke up. "Proud of all the Tuttles except me..."

"What's wrong, Brock?" Grandma asked.

"Well... everyone always talks about how Tuttles do important things and that they stand up for what's right," he said. "I've heard it my whole life."

Brock took a bite of pie before continuing. "My siblings are all successful, but what am I supposed to do? Even Ethan and Emily seem to have life all figured out, and they're way younger than me! So what's my problem?"

The twins felt a bit awkward to be put in the middle of the drama. They were also confused since they looked up to Brock. He often taught them useful wilderness skills and fun wildlife facts.

"In school, my teachers always told me what I was supposed to do, but since I graduated I feel like I don't have any direction in my life," Brock admitted.

"I've got an idea!" Grandpa said, tapping his finger on the side of his head. A moment later he returned with a small notebook, the kind that Grandma used for writing down her recipes.

He handed Brock the notebook and a pen. "You want to create a good life, right?" he asked. "Well, like this delicious pie, you need a recipe. And just now you already discovered three ingredients!"

"I did?" Brock asked in surprise. "What did I do except complain in front of everybody?"

"You shared your true feelings," Mrs. Tuttle said. "You were honest with yourself and with us."

"And that's how relationships are built," Mr. Tuttle said, taking her hand. "On trust—whether it's with family, friends, your community, or in business."

"Without a foundation of trust, there is chaos. We'd all be confused and frustrated—not knowing how to make things better," Grandpa said. "There's your first ingredient—your first rule for life!"

Brock wrote *Tell the truth* in his new recipe book. "I guess I didn't want you to worry about me or think I was dumb," he said. "I should have trusted you more to share what I was feeling."

② Communicate precisely

"And that leads to the second rule," Grandpa continued. "Because Brock shared his troubles so honestly and precisely, we can share our experiences and wisdom to help him overcome his challenges. The second rule is to communicate precisely."

Brock wrote *Communicate precisely*. "Seems simple enough," he said, looking at his short list. "What's the third thing?"

Grandpa sat back down in his chair, looking first at the twins, and then at Brock. After a slow breath, he cracked a grin and said, "That's where my big idea comes in."

"No one can be expected to know everything. So there's no shame in learning valuable lessons from others," Grandpa continued. "That's a lesson itself—and one you need to learn, Son."

Brock began writing *Learn from others* in his recipe book.

"That's why I want the twins here to teach you the rest of the rules."

"What?" Brock replied in unison with Ethan and Emily.

"Being open to learning requires us to be humble and realize there might be something to learn from anyone," Grandma shared. "This sounds like a fun idea to me! What do you all say?"

"Kinda feels weird... but sure," Brock shrugged.

Though intimidated at first, the twins were excited to help and spent the rest of the day brainstorming about other rules that might help Brock.

③ Learn from others

"Atten... TION!" Brock was startled awake by Ethan's shouting and Emily's attempt at playing a bugle. Illuminated by a small amount of light coming from the budding sunrise, he saw that the twins were dressed up like drill sergeants.

Brock looked over at the clock. It read 5:30 in the morning. "What's happening...?" he groggily asked.

"Welcome to the 12 Rules Boot Camp!" Ethan said. "Grandma says there are twelve ingredients in her pie. So we've got twelve rules to get your life on track."

"Wait, now there are twelve?" Brock whined. "This is going to take forever!"

"Quiet, maggot!" Emily shouted back so harshly that Brock actually jumped in surprise. "Just kidding. I've just always wanted to say that."

"For the next three days, you're committed to us!" Ethan tossed a piece of tin on a string to his uncle. It was a homemade dogtag featuring his name, *Brock Tuttle.*

11

Brock's two drill sergeants ordered him to get ready, but he requested permission to feed his dog, Barker, and backyard chickens first.

When Brock returned, Ethan shook his head at him. "If only you cared for *yourself* the way that you care for your animals. That starts today, recruit!"

Brock was led to the kitchen where he was ordered to make a healthy breakfast with fruit and protein. "This sugary junk is hereby banned!" Ethan said, throwing Brock's favorite cereal in the trash. "You wouldn't feed this junk to your pets, right?"

"Now brush your teeth!" Emily said, timing him with her stopwatch. "Small circles! Get those gums!"

"From now on you need to take better care of yourself!" Ethan added, handing Brock his recipe book. "That's your next rule."

Brock realized how poorly he ate and how little he exercised. (No wonder he felt crummy...) He wrote *Take care of myself, too* on his list of rules.

④ Take care of
myself, too

It was still quite early in the morning, but Brock couldn't remember the last time he felt more energized and motivated for the day ahead.

"March!" Ethan shouted. The trio stepped in rhythm down the porch steps and to the path that followed the river, along which the twins had planned a series of obstacles.

They spent hours balancing on fallen logs, climbing rocks, and swinging on the big rope over the river. Ethan and Emily did their best to perform each task as well as their uncle, but he was taller and stronger. Brock even defeated them in a 2-on-1 mud ball war.

It was a very fun morning, but Brock was unsure what rule the twins were trying to teach him.

"How is any of this supposed to help me create a better life?" Brock asked, rinsing mud off his arms. He climbed onto a rock where Ethan and Emily were.

"Today you were better than us at those obstacles," Emily stated. "But did we complain about it?"

"Well, no..." Brock replied. "I guess not."

"But last night, you compared yourself to friends, your siblings... and even to us," Ethan said. "The truth is that there will always be people better at certain things than you. Instead, you should only compare yourself to how *you* did in the past," Ethan added.

Brock swam back to shore, grabbed his recipe book, and wrote down the new rule, *Don't compare myself to others*. "I feel better today than I did yesterday," he said. "I guess the rules are working?"

Emily shot him a thumbs up. "Every day, be a little bit better than the last. Make good daily habits, and eventually you will have created an awesome life!"

⑤ Don't compare myself to others

Brock lay on the sand and took in a deep breath of fresh air. The sun was warm on his face, and the sound of the river calmed him. Now that he was focused on improving his life, he also started to appreciate how good his life already was.

"It's easy to complain about what's difficult," Brock said quietly. "And there *are* things I can do to improve it... but really, there's a lot of good already."

Emily smiled, seeing Brock having a better attitude than the day before, and they weren't even halfway through the list!

"Twelve jumping jacks, recruit!" Ethan shouted. Brock jumped up and started. "That's for peeking at the next rule on the list!"

"But... I didn't!" Brock protested.

"Oh?" Ethan replied. "Well then that's quite a coincidence—because taking time to appreciate the good things in life is the next rule!"

Brock threw a playful punch at his nephew, then wrote *Pause to appreciate* in the notebook, thinking of a few things he was grateful for: his health, their home by the river, his animals, and his family.

⑥ Pause to appreciate

Early the next morning, the twins crept into Brock's room. It looked like a bomb had gone off. Stuff was strewn everywhere.

"Rise and shine, sleeping beauty!" Ethan bellowed while Emily started on the bugle.

"Yesterday, you learned about taking care of yourself," Ethan said as Brock rubbed his eyes. "Today, you're going to take on the world!"

"Before you do that," Emily said, holding up a dirty sock, "you need to clean your room! But first—"

"Wait! I know this," Brock interrupted her. "First I need to take care of myself."

He fed his pets, then ate a healthy breakfast and brushed his teeth. The twins gave one another a high five, happy that their boot camp was working.

When Brock returned, Ethan and Emily had written a cleaning checklist on a whiteboard for him.

"I'm guessing there's some sort of boot camp lesson here, right?" he asked the twins.

"Of course, dirtbag!" Ethan shouted, a little louder than planned. "If you want to bring order into your world, you need to be able to create order in your own room. Look at this place!"

Brock's shoulders sank. The twins were right. His bedroom was as chaotic and cluttered as his life was—no plan and barely useable... and it stunk!

"I want this room so clean," Emily commanded, whacking a stick to the checklist, "that I can make a sandwich on the floor—do you hear me?"

"Yes, drill sergeants!" Brock said, dutifully saluting.

When they returned hours later to check on him, Brock's room was impressively clean!

"Mission complete," Ethan said, fist bumping his sister. "Time for the next phase of the boot camp. Brunch!"

Uncle Ben drove Brock and the twins to Thusnelda's, a local diner and family favorite.

"I think I understand that rule now," Brock told them. "It's not just about bedrooms, right? It's about proving to myself that I can make a difference by first starting with what I can control."

Brock handed the twins his recipe book, showing the rule he had written down. *Take control of myself before taking on the world*.

⑦Take control of myself before taking on the world

"This boot camp has been good for me so far," Brock told his older brother, Ben. "I've learned some important things from these little taskmasters." He turned back toward them. "What do you say, guys? Now that my room is clean, am I ready to take on the world?" A big grin crossed his face.

The car stopped in front of the diner. Thusnelda—or Tess, as everyone called her—stood at the entrance with a mop and bucket. "Hi, Tuttles," she said to the group. "Brock, ready to get started?"

"Wait, what?" he asked, first looking at Tess, then at the twins. His grin was gone. "I thought we were here for brunch?"

"*We* are here for brunch. You're here to work," Emily replied.

"This is a boot camp, mophead!" Ethan said. "Do what your new boss tells you!"

Ben and the twins ordered pancakes, a skillet, and smoothies while Brock began mopping the bathroom and cleaning the toilets and sinks. "This isn't fair," he said. "I don't like this at all—it's gross. All I want to do is go home and play video games."

Tess laughed. "Honey, hard work isn't what's making you unhappy. Take a break and eat. I'll let you in on a secret to loving hard work and living a great life!"

Tess sat Brock down, placing in front of him a healthy omelette, sausage links, and a glass of juice. Brock's mood lightened.

"Do you ever feel bored?" Tess asked him.

"Sure. All the time," he replied, stuffing a bite in his mouth. "So I play video games, hang out with friends, and try to have fun to pass the time."

"Would you say that focusing on your own gratification like that leaves you feeling fulfilled or empty?" Tess wondered.

Brock recognized that spending his days seeking the next thrill or good feeling hadn't left him feeling very happy at all.

"Empty," Brock answered. "Like nothing I do really matters. So does hard work fix that?"

Tess answered with another question. "Did working in my bathrooms make you happy?"

"No. It was boring and no fun at all."

Tess shook her head. "I didn't think so. You see, hard work itself isn't the source of happiness," she replied. "But finding meaning in the work might be. For example: I like to cook..."

"Mm-hmm, this is really good..." Brock said, drinking some orange juice. He was in food heaven.

"But what really motivates me is how it's making you feel right now," she chuckled. "My customers appreciate me, and my restaurant brings friends and family together. That's the real purpose of my work... and I'm never bored!"

Brock finished his meal and started sweeping the dining room floor. "I think that's what I've been missing. I'm not really doing anything meaningful with my time and talents."

"Excuse me…" A woman with a young daughter stepped up to their table. "The bathrooms here are always so clean. I appreciate that. Thank you!"

When she walked away, Tess winked at Brock. "No, thank *you*, Brock."

Suddenly Ethan appeared out of nowhere. "Congratulations, Bathroom Boy. Give yourself twelve jumping jacks as a reward!"

Brock began jumping, a big grin erupting across his face. He felt proud—and happy—to do something meaningful to help Tess and her customers.

The Tuttles then waved goodbye and drove away. Brock wrote *Do meaningful things* in his recipe book to remember the rule.

⑧ Do meaningful things

Grandma sat with Brock who had collapsed on the couch after returning home. "Thusnelda called to tell me what you did today. I'm proud of you, Son."

Brock had been doing hard and meaningful things all day. He was exhausted but didn't complain. Tess was really onto something with that last rule. He actually felt happy.

"Mom, it was only cleaning... imagine what I could do if I was good at something special! But all I'm really good at is football and fishing."

"Well, I always enjoyed watching you play football," she said. "And sometimes you bring fish home for dinner. Those are meaningful to me."

"I know, Mom," he said. "But I feel like I need a bigger purpose. I need to learn new skills."

The rest of the family gathered into the living room to join the conversation.

"Were you always good at football?" Grandma Tuttle asked Brock. "Or fishing?"

"No way. Coach made me practice to build muscle and increase speed. Getting tackled hurt, but that just made me want to work even harder to improve."

"Remember when I taught you how to bait a hook? Over and over, you'd throw the line into the water, and the worm would fall off," Grandpa said, laughing.

Brock smiled. "I would ask you to do it for me, but you would always say..."

His brothers all joined in to finish the sentence. "Doing it wrong teaches you how to do it right." They all laughed together, thinking of the thousands of times they had heard that growing up.

"There's your next rule!" Emily said. "Whatever skill you want to master, you can't be afraid to fail at first."

"And failure is a great teacher!" Ethan added. "You can learn when you mess up and try again."

Brock wrote *Don't be afraid to fail* in his notebook.

⑨ Don't be afraid to fail

"Last day of boot camp!" Ethan shouted, walking into Brock's room early the next morning. But Brock was nowhere to be found. He wasn't in his room, out feeding the animals, or anywhere in the house.

When Grandma woke up, the twins asked her if she knew where Brock was. "I believe that's him right there," she said sorrowfully, pointing out the front window.

A police car had stopped out front, and suddenly there was a loud knock at the front door. Grandma Tuttle opened it, revealing her son and his police officer escort.

"Ma'am, your son and his friends were caught vandalizing private property last night," the officer said. "We held him overnight, but the property owner chose not to press charges, so he's all yours."

"I don't see what the big deal is," Brock said. "There's nothing to do in this town... we were just trying to have a little fun."

"That doesn't sound like the son I raised," Grandpa Tuttle said, shaking his head. Brock felt the sting of his father's disappointment.

The police officer handed Brock's items to Grandma, got back in his vehicle, and left. She opened Brock's small notebook to the list he had been writing and showed it to him.

"Which of these rules were you following last night?" she asked him.

Brock was staring at the ground, not wanting to look anyone in the eye. "None of them, I guess," he quietly said.

The family was all awake now and sat on the porch as Brock continued talking about what had happened the previous night.

"I didn't want to spray paint that wall at first, but the group I was hanging out with seemed like they were having fun, and I wanted them to like me," Brock explained. "So I joined in... it was a dumb, meaningless thing to do. I'm sorry."

Grandpa put his hand on Brock's shoulder. "Well, Son... like I always say..."

A faint smile cracked on Brock's face. "Doing it wrong teaches you how to do it right."

"And boy did you do it wrong!" Ethan exclaimed, teasing his uncle. The family laughed, thankful to release some of the tension.

"Sounds like the recruit is ready for the next rule," Emily said, waving Uncle Ben closer.

"Let me show you something," Ben said, sitting next to Brock. He showed him the contact list on his phone. "This is my network."

"The people who surround you help shape who you become," he added. "Your friends, colleagues, acquaintances, and your family... other people have a big influence on you, whether you realize it or not. If you create a bad network, you'll get bad results and won't reach your full potential."

"That's why we always try to be careful about who our friends are," Emily said. "And we like meeting interesting people who can teach us and help us do important things."

"Or get us out of jail if we're ever arrested," Ethan added, winking at Brock.

Brock scrolled the contacts on his own phone. "Looking at these people... lots of them are nice or whatever, but most of them aren't encouraging me to live a better life," he said. "How do I create a good network?"

⑩ Keep good company

"Brock, you already have a good network," Grandpa said. "Your family. We're all here to support you."

"And we have our own life experience that you can learn from to help you succeed," Grandma added.

"Maybe I can grow my network by borrowing yours?" Brock joked, reaching for Ben's phone.

"Not so fast! Maybe you can after you master these rules for life!" Ben said, tapping the recipe book next to Brock. "But you just came home in a cop car! That doesn't encourage me to introduce you to my friends and colleagues yet."

Brock thought a moment about what he had just been through and learned from his family.

Keep good company, he wrote. The twins nodded in approval then had Brock get ready for the next rule.

"Shhhh!" Ethan whispered to Brock, whose footstep had snapped a twig.

They were all in camouflage observing a herd of deer. "See the one with big antlers?" he asked, passing Brock the binoculars. "It's the leader."

In the hayloft of the barn, they spied on chickens. "Notice the pecking order?" Ethan observed. "They are all hens, but some get their way more often."

They snorkeled around the river looking for crawdads. "See how one is taking the food first?" Emily pointed out. "It's more dominant than others and gets first dibs."

"I'm still confused what any of this has to do with my rules?" Brock later asked as they dried off.

"In each of these groups, there's a ranking, right?" Ethan explained. "The ones at the top get more food and become stronger. This isn't always because they are born that way—mostly it's how they present themselves, which affects how others treat them."

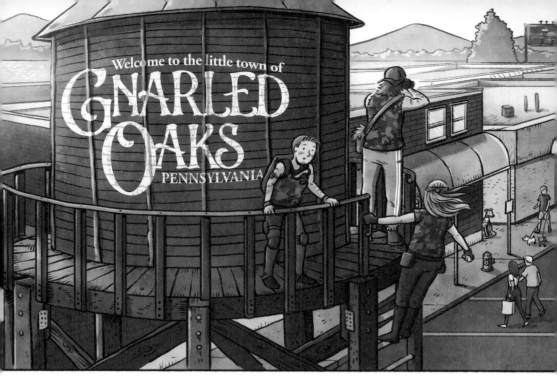

The trio sneaked through town pretending to be spies in enemy territory and then climbed up an old water tank where they could see Main Street below.

"Humans *are* different than other animals," Ethan explained. "But still, the way we dress and act is a signal to others about what kind of person we are and what they should think about us."

"Look at the people," Emily said. "What do you see?"

Brock peered down where people were milling around. "I see a farmer," he said, "with a big truck, overalls, and dirty boots."

"And what does that tell you about him?" Emily asked.

"That he works hard, I guess? Oh look, there's Skater Scott, sporting his... uh, unique style."

"Is it safe to say that Scott wants the reputation of being a rebel?" Ethan wondered.

Brock chuckled, nodding in agreement. "Look. There's a businesswoman," he said. "She also has decorative feathers in her hair... Native American? She's expressing that she's proud of her heritage."

Ethan grabbed the binoculars and used them to look at Brock. "So how are you presenting yourself?"

"Like the animals we saw, people make a reputation for themselves, which creates different opportunites in their life," Emily explained. "What do you want *your* reputation to be?"

"You need to imagine who you want to be in the future," Ethan said, "and then start acting like that person today. That changes how others think about and treat you."

At the twins' prompting, Brock wrote *Act like my best self* in his recipe book.

"There's something I need to do," he said as he led them down to the shop where he had vandalized the alley wall. He apologized to the owner and arranged a time to help clean it up. The owner shook Brock's hand firmly and expressed his gratitude.

"C'mon, twinners," Brock said, exiting the shop. "I want to get a haircut and some new clothes."

⑪ Act like my best self

That night, the Tuttle clan gathered around the fire pit, enjoying more peach pie and ice cream. The twins emerged from behind a curtain on the porch, dressed in their drill sergeant costumes.

Emily's loud bugling brought everyone to attention, and Ethan shouted, "Presenting, our boot camp graduate!"

Brock came out of the house dressed in his new clothes with a fresh haircut. Oohs and aahs carried through the air as his family members admired the change.

"I just want to say again that I'm sorry for what happened last night," Brock said. "This boot camp has helped me realize how much I need to work on myself. And today the twins helped me think about the person I want to be in the future."

"And that's the person I'm going to try to be, starting right now," he added. "I want to live up to the Tuttle family's reputation to help make the world a better place."

"That leads to the twelfth and final rule!" Ethan said. Emily shot off a few more notes on the bugle.

Brock pulled the recipe book out of his pocket. *Bring honor to my family*, he wrote.

"Know what else will bring you honor?" Ethan asked. "Pushups! Down and give me twelve, graduate!"

Brock couldn't resist laughing though every pushup.